"The only time that being invisible could be a bad thing is if the people that matter most can't see you" –Chris Robinson

CONTENTS

CHAPTER 1: What If?

Let's consider a scenario: You woke up feeling fine and your day has been going well thus far. Work was going smooth and even enjoyable for once. The only depressing moment was a news report playing during your lunch. You decide to ignore it and enjoy the work-related conversation because at least it was not that depressing. You get a text sometime during the day; your best friend wants to know if you are going to go walking around town after work. Work is finished, and you are ready for that walk. You and your friend meet up and enjoy each other's company. Suddenly, you hear BANG! BANG! ; Followed by the sound of glass breaking, car alarms and multiple voices chanting in unison. You both round the corner only to be face to face with a giant mob of protestors. You can easily see the protest has turned from peaceful to violent. Cars and garbage cans are on fire; store windows are shattered. Before you know what is happening, you and your friend are surrounded by rioters. Your path back to your vehicles and safety is now blocked. You can see cops moving in to respond. Your fear starts compounding. You ask yourself is there anything I can do? What if the rioters attack us? What if we get caught in the middle of the police deploying pepper spray and flash bangs?

It is a scary scenario to think about, but sadly an increasing reality. How do you answer the previous questions when facing an imminent threat? How do you react? After completing this book, you will have some insight into shadow tactics, and an understanding of how only changing a few key features could save your life.

First a simple explanation of what shadow tactics are. Shadow tactics were developed from similar skills used by C.I.A., Special Forces, and the F.B.I to blend into crowds. Although different agencies use these types of skills, they are not a secret agent as you might think. No need for face masks or other unique gadgets, just your brain and whatever is in your pockets or backpack. We will go into greater depth in later chapters on how to properly execute and prepare for shadow tactics.

Chapter 2: Blending In

If shadow tactics were merely blending into a crowd, then why even study this? How does someone not blend into a crowd? Why should I want to blend in when society continually says to be yourself and show your uniqueness however you see fit? We are told to be loud, bold, and trendy at every turn; so why change? Personally, I am all for unique and bright, but not when it makes you a target. It is hard to blend into the crowd when you are actively drawing attention by those same traits.

Let's correlate this with the scenario at the beginning of the book. If the protest, for example, were politically motived it would not be a good idea to wear a hat or shirt relating to either of the candidates. If you had chosen to do that, you might be opening yourself up as a target for aggression. Another example, you are from the United States and are traveling abroad to a country that America is not on friendly terms with. You ignore this fact and wear a U.S.A. flag shirt; what do you think will happen? Some may say nothing; others will tell you could be killed; both answers are a possibility. You do not know what could happen until you get in a situation but, why test those waters?

The ability to blend in starts with picking clothing that doesn't draw attention. Shirts and hats in a solid neutral color are always a good choice. You know the typical styles of clothes people in your area are wearing; it is still best to dress like the natives when trying to blend in. Chose clothing styles that are commonplace for your location, and in colors such as black, gray, tan or blue. These colors will not draw undue attention to you. You could also don a hat and a pair of sunglasses. This will hide your hair color and style. It will also cast a shadow over your facial features. Sunglasses amplify this effect even more by covering up eye color and more of the face. Another way of hiding facial features in males would be growing a beard or shaving it off. Females can always change their hairstyle from long to short. Even changing hair color can completely throw off acquaintances.

An actual example of how clothing can get you singled out in a crowd happened to me this past election. My family and I went to the polls to vote. We went early that morning hoping to beat the lines. However, it was a two-hour wait with fifty to hundred people ahead of us in line. It was freezing that morning. We had on coats and hoodies, and I was wearing another state's college basketball team hat. Several people were working the polls and were coming by and talking to everyone, handing out coffee and hot chocolate. After an hour had passed and we might have moved ten feet, the kids have become rambunctious due to boredom, we gave up and said we would come back later. A few hours later my kids and I finally returned. As I finally neared the doors, I was approached by a worker who asked me why I was back. I replied I had left and hadn't voted. I gave him some necessary information so he could verify this to be true. After returning the worker apologized for the misunderstanding, and said: "Sorry, I just remember seeing you here earlier from your basketball teams hat." If I had grabbed a different hat with no markings that morning, he might not have recognized me. I had removed my coat, and my shirt had no identifying markers on it.

So another way of blending in is related to the mind and the body, as they reflect one another. If you are calm and collect your body language will reflect this. If you are stressed your facial features will reveal this so people around you might take notice. You may also appear tense, with flexed and strained muscle. You may even notice a quickened respiratory rate. If you can stay calm your body language will seem more relaxed therefore you will not draw as much attention. A way of achieving this is through the art of suggestion. If you tell yourself something enough your mind will start to believe it, in turn, your body will reflect it.

Another helpful tip is to be aware of the people around you, or situational awareness. If you are aware of what people around you are doing it will lend you vital information to help blend in. The more information you gather, the quicker and easier it will be to get out of dodge. Take the scenario at the beginning; if you had stopped and listened to what the rioters were screaming, you would have enough details about their cause to become "part of the protest." You could then merely blend in by chanting and following the movement of the crowd until you can safely break away. If that is the option that you chose to take, you should not engage in many conversations as this could blow your cover. During your progress to safety observe people's hands and body language. This could help alert you to danger. Hands are a big key to identifying possible threats as they can either control the weapons or are the weapons.

Please note that this isn't the ideal strategy but if it's the only option you have to use it. Be aware it does possess its risks, and you may get caught in the police response. Always take the first open and safe way out. To help facilitate this hang towards the outside of the crowd this way you can break off with no one noticing, but also keeps you away from the possible vandalism happening on the outer most portion of the riot.

With these simple tactics, you can enter and exit a riot without drawing attention to yourself. You will be able to gather information to help you blend in and also to spot possible threats. The question now is what happens when there is a threat?

CHAPTER 3: IT'S OK TO RUN AWAY

As a child, I was always told I should never start a fight but, I should finish it. To this day I still agree with that statement, but sometimes it is better just to walk away. Be prepared to defend yourself if the situation so arises; however, the point is to get out of these conditions without getting hurt or calling attention to yourself. Running away is a very preferred option and could save yours or someone else's life. It is not cowardly to choose the safest opportunity given to you.

When running is not an option, it is best to practice cover and concealment (C.and C.). Cover and concealment is a hiding and protective technique. Anyone who has taken a defensive gun course will already know the basics of this method, but you can practice them even if you do not have a weapon. Cover is a barrier that protects you from dangers such as bullets. Concealment, on the other hand, hides you from view but does not stop bullets if shot in your direction. By being aware of your environment (environmental awareness), you will be able to identify potential C. and C. barriers.

For example, cover would be the big concrete flower pot you see on sidewalks in towns or at malls; while concealment would be hiding behind the mall directory sign. It is not strong enough to stop a bullet, but they will have a hard time seeing you there.

A real-life scenario incorporates topics from this chapter is as follows. My elderly father and his friend attended a college basketball game. The parking was limited, so they parked in a garage roughly two blocks away from the arena. On the way to the stadium, they found themselves surrounded by protestors marching down the streets. Instead of pushing through the crowd of demonstrators the friend noticed a bar just a little way from their current location. They followed the group until they reached the bar, where they were able to wait until the protesters passed. They could have attempted to push through to the arena, but that could have opened them up to aggression if things turned violent. Instead, they used environmental awareness and found cover and concealment in a bar.

CHAPTER 4: EVERYDAY CARRY AND OTHER FUN KITS

In this chapter, we will discuss a few tools to aid with shadow tactics. We will talk about everyday carry (E.D.C.), get home bags (G.H.B.) and individual first aid kit (I.F.A.K.) and how they relate to shadow tactics.

Everyday carry kits are very simple. It is the items that you never leave the house without; this can vary from person to person. I will give you an example of my E.D.C.: wallet, keys, cell phone, pocket knife, a cigarette lighter, flashlight, pistol, inside the waistband (I.W.B.) pistol holster, two extra magazines for the gun, two inside the waistband (I.W.B.) magazine holsters, and a watch. E.D.C.'s can be anything. I tend to follow these two rules when deciding my E.D.C. 1) Can it fit on or in my pants comfortably and 2) will it draw attention? When selecting what to carry regarding weapons, I would not choose a massive gun to conceal. The smaller the print, the better; an example of firearms leaving an impression would be a large handgun which could be spotted quickly depending on what you are wearing versus a compact or subcompact which could leave a small to nonexistent imprint on your clothing. My E.D.C. changes depending on the situation and location of my journey. Always know the state and local laws relating to Concealed deadly weapons, if you so choose to carry a gun.

Get home bags (G.H.B.) is a little more advanced from an E.D.C. and is essentially extra support items. G.H.B's can be any shoulder bag. My G.H.B consists of these things and change depending on what I anticipate to encounter. My suggestion for a G.H.B. includes a simple school backpack(in a neutral color). Long sleeve shirt or zip up hoody, an entire change of clothes (depending); I.F.A.K.; one to two bottles of water; paracord; extra batteries for my flashlight; extra lighter; extra ammo for my pistol; and a portable cell phone charger and cord. I follow this simple rule when building a get home bag; what else would I need to get to safety that can't fit on my person without drawing attention.

I.F.A.K.'S or individual first aid kits are always good to have. You never know when you or a loved one may get hurt. You can build your own or buy one pre-stocked. Beware that the pre-stocked ones can run you some money. This is an example of my I.F.AK.: burn relief gel, 7 inch safe trauma shears, CPR mask, couple sets of exam gloves, alcohol preps, assorted waterproof bandages, self-adherent cohesive wrap bandage, cortisone cream, conforming stretch gazes, butterfly closures, 3 inch compression bandage, 4x4 gaze, antihistamine, ibuprofen, chapstick and a compact pouch 8x6x3 inches (L x W x T). All these items can be purchased at local stores or online. When building your I.F.A.K., you

should ask what is my medical training level than stock it accordingly.

EXAMPLE OF AN EDC

EXAMPLES OF AN I.F.A.K.

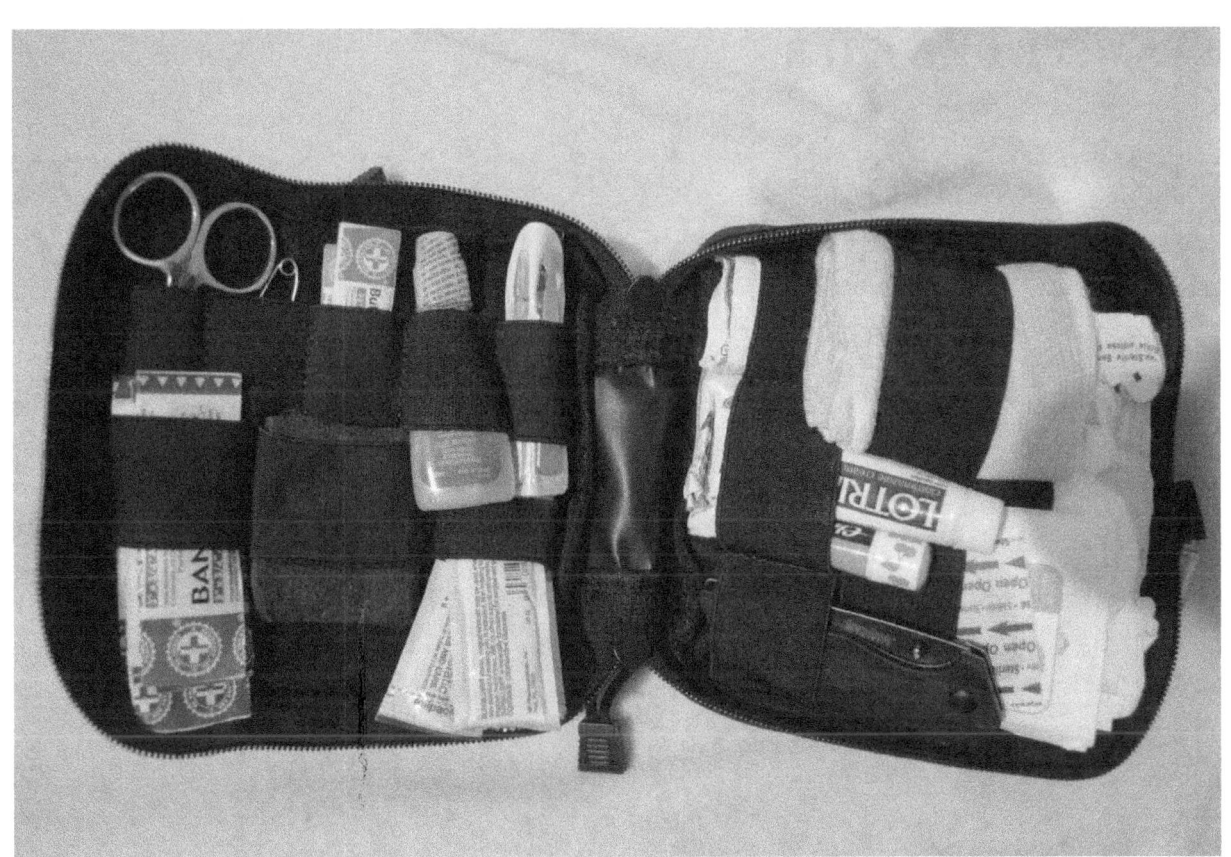

EXAMPLE OF A G.H.B

CHAPTER 5: TRAINING FOR THE FINISH LINE

An excellent instructor once told me that training out ways gear every time. This is one of the most important statements ever said to me. You can buy the best equipment out there, but if you do not have the training and skills to use it, the gear is useless. With the proper training, you will have the upper hand in most situations.

Hand to Hand fighting techniques are an excellent area to start. Your body can be a weapon. Mastering a fighting style can save you from harm in many situations. In my opinion, it is essential to pick a hand to hand form that is a mix fighting style. This can prepare you for ground and upright fights. It is imperative that you choose a method that you enjoy and will suit your needs.

What if you need more than your body to protect yourself? Weapons' training can also be important especially if you chose to carry a firearm. If you choose to carry, a firearm, take that particular weapon to all your firearm training classes. That way you will be familiar with that weapon, and it will help you build muscle memory. Most traditional fighting styles have some form of weapon's training; which can aid in your skills with a knife if you so choose to carry one. Other alternatives to consider besides lethal weapons are non-lethal weapons such as a Taser or pepper spray etc. You may never need to draw a gun but if you do training with that weapon can save your life.

Medical training has a role in any situation. I am not saying you have to become an E.M.T. or physician but knowing basic CPR and first aid will always come in handy. C.P.R and first aid are basic entry level classes taught in one afternoon. It will impart unto you the knowledge to use everything in your I.F.A.K.

Before traveling to a foreign country, it would be wise to learn their customs and language. This is not limited to going abroad. There are many multilingual locations within the United States. Communication is the key to finding your way to safety. I would recommend being fluent in the most common language spoken in the area you are traveling. There are numerous language software's available. You can learn a language in your free time right from your phone, in most cases. Being able to defend, heal, and communicate will allow you to address the situation by whatever means you have determined.

CHAPTER 6: LET'S TIE IT A

ltogether

It is up to you to figure out what gear you feel is best in aiding you to blend in and keep safe. The key to surviving any situation while using shadow tactics is a mixture of becoming a phantom in the crowd and fighting your way out if the worse does happen. Having the weapons and hand to hand training aids you if the ability to blend in has failed, and you have no other way out of a violent situation. Always remember to stay calm think it through and take note of the people and structures around you. Still, the fastest and safest way out of danger. Do not draw attention to yourself and don't engage the threat if you can avoid it. Thank you for reading this book. I hope it has helped answer some questions or at least gave you a place to start preparing for these types of situations. Stay safe, and God bless.

GLOSSARY

C. & C.-Cover and Concealment

C.P.R. - Cardiopulmonary Resuscitation

E.D.C.-Everyday carry

E.M.T.-Emergency medical technician

G.B.H.-Get home bag

I.F.A.K.-Individual first aid kit

I.W.B.-Inside the waistband

ABOUT THE AUTHOR

Christopher Robinson was born in Kentucky and currently resides in North

Carolina. He holds certificates in Counter Terrorism, Executive Protection, and

Physical Security. He also holds numerous firearms training and F.E.M.A.

Certifications.

NOTE FROM THE AUTHOR

This book was written in the hopes of informing people. I hope that in the course of reading this book it has helped answer questions about how to survive in certain situations. Books are a great way to learn, but training with a certified instructor is always recommended. Thank you for choosing my book. There are many other great books to supplement your education. I hope that my book was enjoyable to read and again thank you, the reader, for choosing this book. As always stay safe and stay prepared.

SPECIAL THANKS

I want to thank Peg, Cameron, Abby, my parents, and my friends and family for always supporting me. I'd also like to thank Sisco, you know who you are, for your training and help that has brought me this far. To Arwyn, Letisha, Matthew, LaDonna, and Peg, thank you guys for the grammar checks and reading this book over and over again. I really couldn't have done this without all of your support, thank you all so much. Also, thank you to the reader this book was for you.